The Nature Kid's Guide to
BADGERS

DAVID ANDERSON

LP Media Inc. Publishing
Text copyright © 2026 by LP Media Inc.
All rights reserved.

For information address LP Media Inc. Publishing,
30012 Variolite St NW, Princeton MN 55371
www.lpmedia.org

Publication Data

Badgers
The Nature Kid's Guide to Badgers — First edition.

Summary: "Learn all about Badgers, the Nature Kid Way"
— Provided by publisher.

ISBN: 979-8-89818-157-4

[1. Badgers – Non-Fiction] I. Title.

Title: The Nature Kid's Guide to Badgers

CONTENTS

BURROW BUILDERS

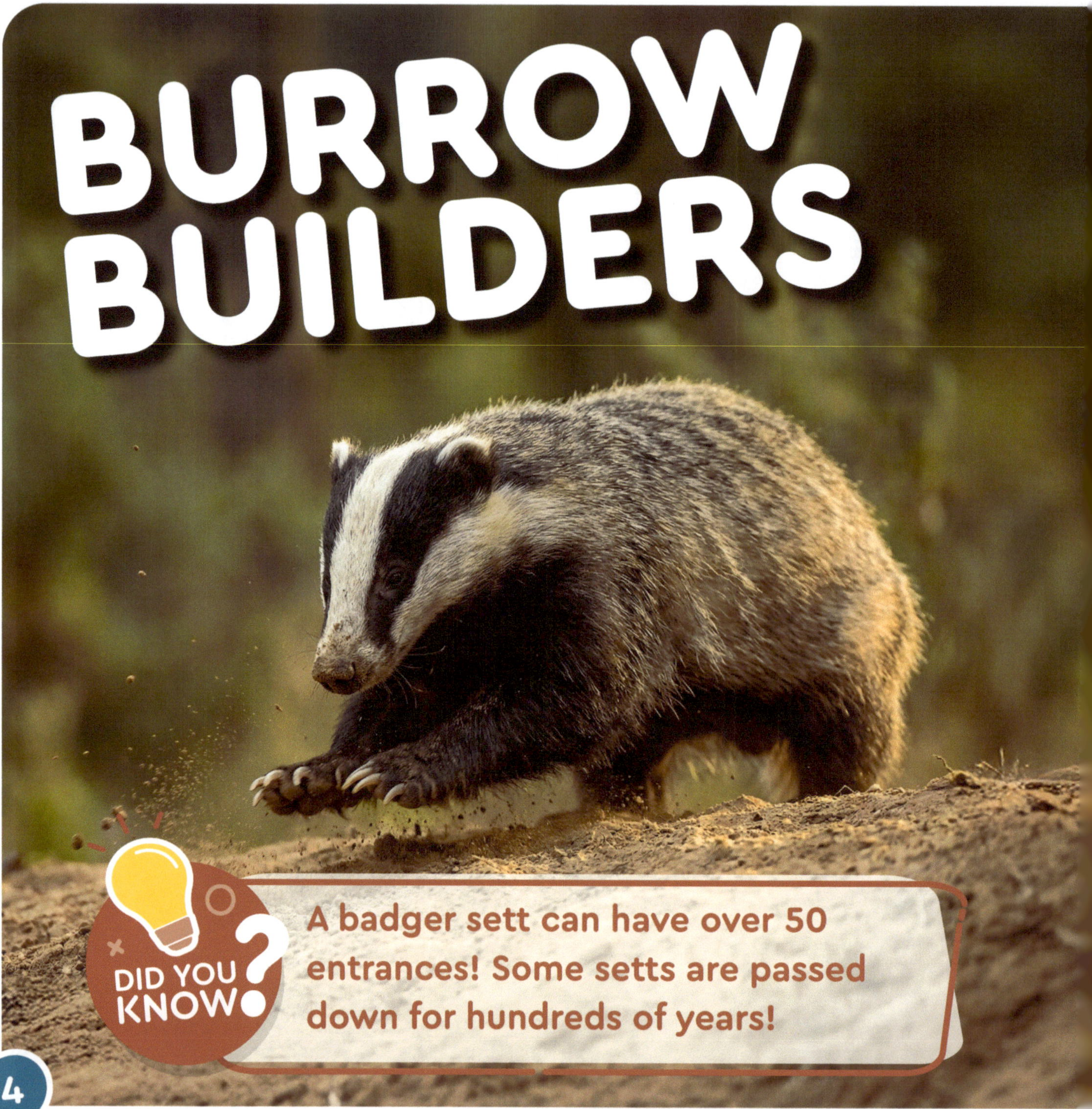

DID YOU KNOW?

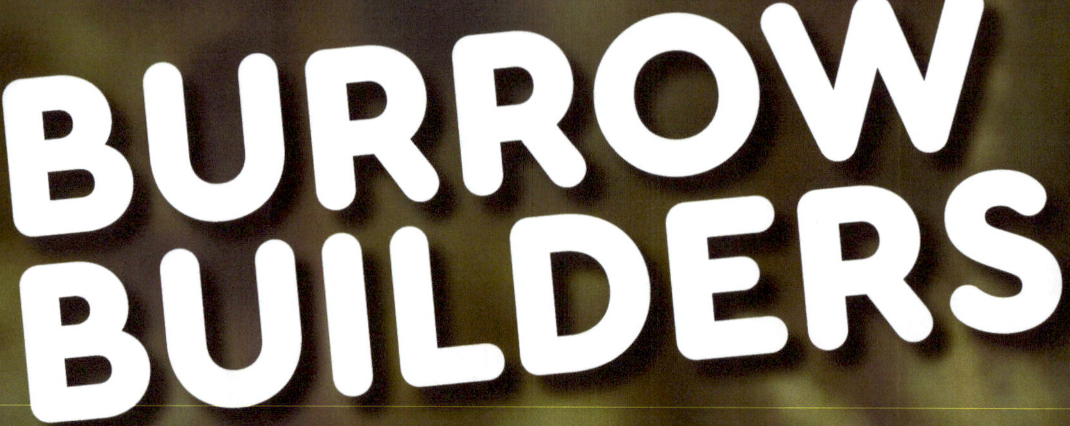

A badger sett can have over 50 entrances! Some setts are passed down for hundreds of years!

Scratch! A badger digs into soft, sandy soil. Its strong claws move fast.

Badgers need to live in places with loose, dry ground. They dig deep tunnels called **setts**. Soft earth lets them build tunnels that become their homes.

These animals like open areas. Grasslands and meadows work well. Some badgers live in forests with clearings. They need space to hunt at night.

Badgers pick spots with sloping ground so water does not flood their tunnels. The ground stays dry inside their burrows.

Badgers like mild weather but some do live in hot deserts. Cold winters are fine too because setts stay warm underground.

BADGER MAP

European badgers can run backward into their dens. This helps them get away from danger!

Snort! A European badger pokes its striped face out of a hole.

European badgers live in Europe and Asia. They live from Britain to Russia. Many live in forests. Many live on farm land.

American badgers live in North America. They are found from southern Canada down to Mexico. They are most common in the wide open plains and grasslands of the western United States.

Honey badgers live in Africa and parts of Asia. They are the toughest of all badgers and are famous for being fearless.

Hog badgers live in the forests of Southeast Asia. They get their name from their pig-like snouts, which they use to root around in the dirt for food.

STOCKY
STRIPERS

Thump! An American badger waddles across a field. It looks small but heavy.

Badgers are short and wide. They stand only about 12 inches tall, but they are heavy!

American badgers weigh about 25 lbs. on average, that's the size of a lot of dogs! European badgers can weigh even more.

From nose to tail, badgers measure about 30 inches long. Picture two bowling pins end to end. That is how long a badger can be!

Badgers have loose, baggy skin. This helps them twist and bite back if grabbed!

BUILT TOUGH

10

Growl! A badger shows its sharp teeth. Its body is built for digging.

Badgers have thick, loose skin. This helps them twist away from bites. Their coarse, wiry fur adds extra protection too.

Badgers also have long, curved claws. Front claws can grow over one inch long! These work like shovels for digging.

Badgers have small ears and tiny eyes. Their small ears fold flat against their heads. This keeps dirt out when they dig.

Their teeth are strong and sharp. Powerful jaws help them crunch through tough food.

SUPER
SNIFFERS

Sniff! An American badger lifts its nose to the air. What does it smell?

Badgers have an amazing sense of smell. Their long snouts hold millions of scent cells. This helps them find food buried underground!

Badgers smell about 800 times better than humans. They sniff out worms, bugs, and mice hiding in the dirt.

Badger eyes are small and weak. But their super noses make up for it!

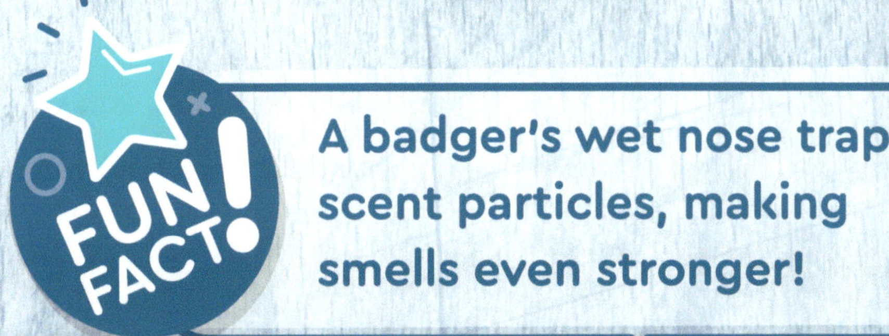

BOLD
BADGES

Hiss! A predator approaches. The European badgers bold stripes say "stay away"!

Badgers have black and white stripes on their faces. These bold markings warn other animals. The stripes say this animal is tough!

Badger colors help them hide too. Their gray backs blend into shadows at night. This makes them hard to see in the dark.

Badgers also have a secret weapon. They spray stinky **musk** from glands near their tails. The smell drives enemies away!

Badger stripes start at birth! Babies are born with their markings already showing.

MIDNIGHT MUNCHIES

Crunch! A badger chomps on a beetle. What a yummy snack!

Badgers eat many different foods. They munch on earthworms, beetles, and grubs. Worms are their favorite snack! One badger can eat hundreds of worms in a single night!

Badgers also eat small animals. They gobble up mice, rabbits, and frogs. They even snatch bird eggs for a tasty treat.

Badgers eat plants as well. They enjoy berries, roots, and corn.

Earthworms make up the largest part of a badger's diet!

DIG DEEP

A badger can dig itself completely underground in less than one minute. Try to beat that with a shovel!

Rustle! A badger digs fast in the grass. Dirt flies everywhere!

Badgers are expert diggers. They use their long, curved claws like shovels. They can dig faster than almost any animal on earth! Their strong front legs help them move dirt quickly.

Badgers hunt by digging into the ground. They follow their noses to find prey hiding below. Then they dig straight down to catch it!

Badgers also dig sideways into burrows. They chase rabbits and ground squirrels right out of their homes. Sometimes badgers dig all night long looking for food.

WATCH OUT

Swoosh! A golden eagle dives from the sky. Below, a badger looks up.

Badgers have some enemies. Golden eagles hunt badger **cubs**. These big birds dive down fast from the sky.

Wolves hunt young badgers too. So do coyotes. They try to catch badgers far from home. Mountain lions are also a threat.

But adult badgers are hard to catch. They fight back with sharp claws. Most predators leave big badgers alone.

A badger can back into its burrow and block the entrance with its tough, thick rear end.

FIGHT BACK

Snarl! A badger turns to face a fox. It stands its ground.

Badgers are brave fighters. They do not run away from danger. Instead, they turn and face their enemies head-on!

Badgers use their sharp claws to fight back. They bite hard with strong jaws. They also make loud hissing and growling sounds.

When scared, badgers puff up their fur. This makes them look bigger. Most animals leave badgers alone!

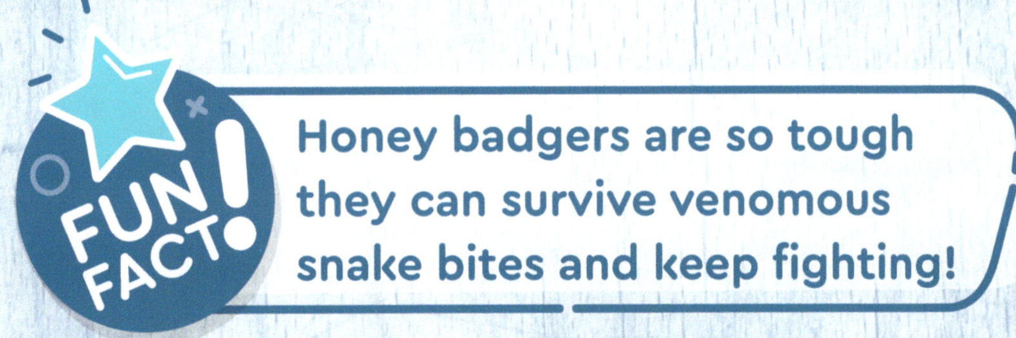

WADDLE WALK

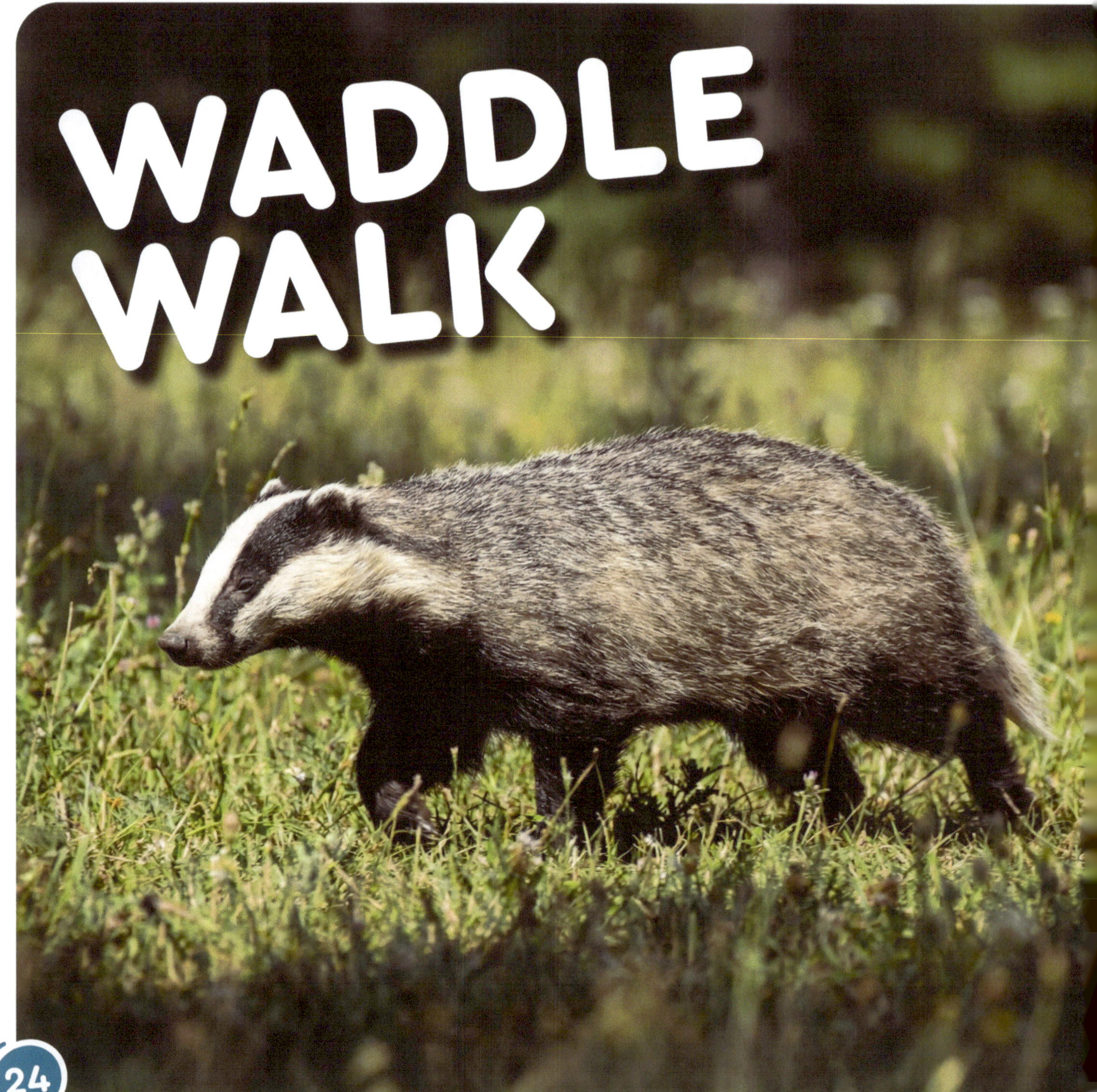

Stomp! A badger walks across a meadow. Its short legs swing side to side.

Badgers waddle when they walk. Their short legs and wide bodies make them sway from side to side. This means they are not built for speed!

Badgers can still run up to 19 miles per hour. But they cannot run fast for long.

When danger comes, they often dig down instead of running away.

Badgers can swim! They paddle with all four legs. But they prefer to stay on dry land.

NIGHT SHIFT

DID YOU KNOW?
Badgers can sleep for up to 29 hours at a time during winter, staying warm in their cozy burrows!

Squeak! A mouse runs through the grass. Nearby, a badger wakes up to hunt.

Badgers are **nocturnal**. This means they sleep during the day and come out at night. They spend most daylight hours resting in their burrows.

At sunset, badgers wake up. They groom their fur and stretch. Then they leave their burrows to find food.

Badgers spend most of the night searching for meals. They return home before sunrise to sleep again.

CLAN LIFE

Grunt! Two badgers touch noses. They sniff hello at their den.

European badgers live in groups. These groups are called **clans**. A clan can have 2 to 23 badgers. They share one big burrow.

One male and one female lead the clan. This female is the main mother.

American badgers. Honey badgers, and Hog badgers are different. They live alone most of the time.

Badger clans have their own bathrooms! They dig pits away from their dens.

FINDING MATES

Chirp! A male badger calls out. It is dark. He wants to find a mate.

Badgers mate at different times. European badgers often mate from February to May. American badgers mate in late summer or early fall.

Male badgers make soft calls. They leave scent marks too. This helps them find a mate.

Female badgers have a neat trick. Their bodies can wait to have babies. This way, cubs come in late winter or early spring.

Male badgers may walk many miles in one night when looking for a female mate to start a family!

CUTE CUBS

DID YOU KNOW?

Newborn badger cubs are about 5 inches long. That is shorter than a pencil! They weigh only 3 to 5 ounces.

Grunt! Tiny cubs peek out of their burrow, they want to explore!

Baby badgers are called cubs. They are born in late winter or early spring. A mother badger usually has 1 to 5 cubs at once.

Newborn cubs are very small. They weigh only about 3 to 5 ounces. That is lighter than a baseball!

Cubs are born with thin, grayish-white fur. Their famous black and white stripes are already visible too. Their eyes stay closed for about 4 to 5 weeks.

GROWING UP

DID YOU KNOW?
A mother badger moves her cubs to a new den if danger comes near.

Snap! A mother badger peeks out of her den. Her cubs are ready to play!

Mother badgers care for their cubs alone. Cubs drink their mother's milk for about 12 weeks. During this time, she keeps them safe deep in the burrow.

The mother teaches cubs how to find food. She shows them how to dig for worms and grubs. Cubs follow her on nighttime trips.

Young badgers stay with their mother for several months. American badger cubs leave by late summer. European cubs may stay with the clan for a year or more.

HONEY BADGERS

Hiss! A cobra rises up. The honey badger does not back down.

The honey badger is the toughest badger in the world. It lives in the hot deserts and grasslands of Africa and Asia.

Honey badgers eat almost anything. They dig up scorpions. They catch venomous snakes. They even raid beehives to eat the bee babies inside. They spray a terrible smell to chase the bees away first.

Honey badgers live alone. They wander from place to place. They sleep in a different burrow almost every night.

HOG BADGERS

Hog badgers can dig so fast that when a tiger gets too close, they disappear underground before it can reach them!

Snuffle. A hog badger walks with it's nose to the dirt. It can smell a worm hiding underground!

The hog badger is the biggest badger in the world. It lives deep in the mountain forests of Southeast Asia. And it has the funniest nose of any badger: long, pink, and shaped just like a pig's snout!

That piggy nose can smell worms and bugs buried underground. Then the hog badger digs them up with its powerful white claws.

It lives alone, wandering the dark forest at night, following its nose wherever it leads.

GLOSSARY

setts
Underground homes with tunnels that badgers dig and live in.

cubs
Baby badgers.

clans
Groups of badgers that live together and share a home.

nocturnal
An animal that sleeps during the day and is awake at night.

musk
A stinky smell that badgers spray to keep enemies away.